THE UNAPOLOGETIC
MOON

E.W. RIGHTINGS

THE UNAPOLOGETIC
MOON

Printed and Electronic Versions
ISBN: 978-1-7340250-8-8
(E.W. Rightings/Motivation Champs)

The book was printed
in the United States of America.

To order additional copies or bulk order contact the publisher,
Motivation Champs Publishing. www.motivationchamps.com

This book is dedicated to my parents.

For my mother who always holds a flashlight for me.

For my father, my favorite star in the sky.

I am forever grateful for you both, for your grace and light.

Love you forever to eternity.

Meet me by the Moon. It's where the wild hearts go to be understood. And no one apologizes for their light.

– E.W.

Dear Friend –

I have always been enamored with the moon. The way it has the ability to light up the night sky, disappear and circle back to its luminosity again. It's always there. Kind of like life. We go through phases. Some days we are as bright as a full moon and other days hiding in the dark until it is our time to shine again.

There are no instructions for reading this. Only to move at your own pace, jump to parts that speak to you or revisit pieces as they read the loudest. I've left some space at the end for your personal reflection to use at your discretion.

Whatever you are going through and wherever you are, know you have a friend in me. All I ask for is when you are ready, shine your light, it's the one thing that can never be stolen from you. Sending you peace for your heart today and always. See you at the moon.

Love,
E.W.

INDEX

Waning Crescent, losing light

New Moon, dark days

Waxing Crescent, gaining light

Full Moon, shining bright

WANING CRESCENT
losing light

FUEL

If only I could have known my fears were your fuel.

AFTERTASTE

His touch was all I hungered for and the aftertaste
was nothing but regret.

BODY LANGUAGE

We spoke two different languages,
that only our bodies could translate.

UNACCEPTED APOLOGY

You stole my truths and twisted them into lies,

so that my truths became my apologies.

CIRCUS CLOWN

I loved the person you pretended to be
and when my brain fantasizes what we had,
I am reminded of the circus we were
and why I am so afraid of clowns.

VACANT HEART

My feet started moving but my heart had not yet
left the home it no longer belonged to.

CHAPPED LIPS

The problem was, I was convinced
every inch of my body was made for your lips.
And your lips agreed.

FERTILIZER

You said I was the most beautiful girl you'd ever seen;

Noting my eyes looked like sunflowers

as we stood in the sun.

Why didn't you water them with love,

instead of my own tears?

COMBUSTION

We were fire signs
Our explosive chemistry written in the stars
But, my fire brought you warmth
Your fire brought me pain.

VACANT HOME

I did not find love in your lies.

They were just a temporary home

of what I wanted to hear.

I had not yet decided who I wanted to be.

I let your words make that decision for me.

PUPPET MASTER

I'm sorry for all the times I blamed you as the puppeteer.
Not for all your wrongdoings,
but on the days I held the strings.

PIRATE'S GOLD

He was purposeful in the way he touched her
His calloused hands tracing every curve,
claiming ownership
Like a pirate stealing golden treasure
Without regard or need for a map.
Where his hands sought purpose with her body,
he was reckless with her heart
Leaving her at night to find shore without a light.
Parched and alone with nothing but
faded memories of a careless touch.

DEVIL'S PLAY

She was a sweet soul
with lustful energy.
And some days she wasn't sure what character to play
But when she was with him
There was no question
She was reading from the devil's script
And she never forgot her lines.

BREADCRUMBS

The fibers in the web you weaved
held me down far too long.
Using me for food when you felt hungry,
Making promises
from the empty vessel you called your soul.
I wasn't much better as I gave you crumbs,
when we both know I'm a whole damn feast.
We both took what we needed,
spitting eight letter words into each other's face
yet showed one another exactly what love wasn't.
Your name is no longer bitter on my tongue
and I'm grateful to have realized you weren't the one.

THE DANCE

She slid off her wings to dance with the devil
despite being afraid of the dark.
He softened his horns while holding her hand,
afraid of her light.
Two bodies, waltzing recklessly
without music but to the song their feet knew by heart.

CHECKMATE

We were completely and utterly addicted to one another

To the outside world we were invincible

We were a façade.

Shiny buildings home to mismatched interiors

Inside our little world we toyed one another

Playing games with broken chess pieces.

Following different rules but still keeping score.

And in the end,

it was a tie on whose heart split the loudest.

I still think I won.

FROZEN

I was stuck in a race between my head and heart
and neither wanted to take the lead.

HEART BREAKER

She didn't believe his lies, but her loneliness did.
So, she continued breaking her own heart,
until one day she realized
lonely and alone
are not one in the same.

SPLINTERED HEARTS

Two lost souls carried by the night
Left with old scars and no regard for light
Only holding on by one another's touch
And for their splintered hearts,
It was more than enough.

LETTERS TO MY FORMER LOVERS

To every lover who could not keep me, it wasn't you.
I, in fact, had not yet found myself.

THIS HOUSE IS NOT A HOME

As he sits and stares at the paint chipped interior
He hears her voice whisper in the walls
"this house is not a home."
A flashback to a conversation gone by.
When did this house fall apart?
Previously complacent with his untruths
because they survived him thus far.
But the reality is truth and untruth don't partner well as they're
both built on different foundations and together, they don't
weather the storm.
They are the storm.
And only one person is left
picking up the damage of the aftermath.
He has questions and longs to connect to that light
that used to shine through the windows,
but it is gone,
And this house is no longer a home.
Oh, the irony of the liar that begs for truth.

OVERSTAYED WELCOME

She stayed in a house for a little too long
Residing in someone's four-walled chambers
where she didn't belong.
I wonder if he would continue to comply,
If he understood that he was supply
For the chemical high of a soul that had run dry
Would he continue to show up and try to love her fully?
If he understood it stemmed from her being lonely
For a heart that just wanted to feel love and alive
But all it could do was try to survive
The pain of a liar in love with someone else's lies
The guilt and the shame held the ties
Which held her down for entirely too long
She wouldn't let go, even though it was wrong.

GHOST OF GUILT

Ghost of guilt and shackle of shame

Left me out to freeze in the rain.

Naked under a dark cloud of doom and despair

Left with only tears in effort to repair

A voice long since silenced by these two

Dragging my feet stuck on you

Avoiding what I need to do

To let go of you so I could be *free*

To let go of you so you could let go of *me*.

LOVE LIES

There came a point in her relationship
which left her wondering,
when we they said I love you to one another,
which one of their tongues held the greater lie?

CROSSING GUARD

He crossed every boundary I had.

Without space for my own breath.

But his line jumping wasn't the worst

I held his hand at the intersection to help him get there.

CON-ARTIST

To the man who took my heart,
painted it with lies and called it love.
Thank you.
You woke the sleeping goddess inside me
She no longer fears her light
You may have caught me with your lies,
but you lost me with my truth.

GUN METAL

Cold metal kissed my temple for what felt like forever
but I'm certain was seconds.
Before my tightly closed eyes flashed moments, memories,
and unchecked bucket lists

My conscious and subconscious mind exchanged
a cyclone of dizzied thoughts
as I toed the very thin line between life and death

Feet on the car floorboard but I viewed my body
from a bird's eye view
Detached from reality but fixated on fear

Was I already dead?
Had the bullet already penetrated my head?

My shaking hand had been milliseconds from
committing my phone from 9-1-1 to send
I could not believe this happened to myself and my friend

I prayed hard, reviewing the life I had led
Would I meet the pearly gates or the man in red?

The pain of my family to learn my life would be a loss
For this coward to only get twenty dollars and
drug store lip gloss?

As he had lost the battle of casino winnings from my friend
But it was my purse he won in the end

My Herculean friend fought off the man with the gun
Until the pistol whipped his face and left him with dripping blood

The man drove off and left my spirits shattered
But when you face down a gun, it's only life that matters
An evening I've tried to push out of my mind

To leave that man and his transgressions far behind me
Time has moved on and I've learned to forget his sight

But I won't forget,
meeting myself at the end of the barrel that night.

GOODBYE OLD LIFE

The sky is red and the ground burning blue

No longer living in the world we knew

Time has stopped and started again

Many wondering what's around this bend

Grieving for a time that used to be

Left wondering was that previous life for me

Time will tell, and we will make do

For now, waving goodbye to the world we once knew

DEAR DAISY

One day would have been too long
You spent five years.
Silenced by a cage, left to sit in your own excrement
with matted fur, and yet your tail still wags.
Some days I try to understand it,
but I can't find ways to make sense of it
I'm sorry.
I cannot explain the cruelties of some two-legged beasts
Some people's hearts grow colder as they grow older,
tainted by a love they never received.
And I don't excuse it, but I recognize it.
In my beliefs we aren't born evil, but our stories shape us
Just like I'm sure yours did you.
And here you are impaired, broken
Yet still so full of love and hope.
Humans have so much to learn from animals.
From here on out, little one, you are safe, you are loved,
and you can leave your past behind.

MASKS

These masks cannot be
anymore obstructive than the ones society already had you wearing.
There was an abhorrent virus walking amongst us
long before the year of vision.
And you didn't want to protect yourself from that one either.

THE VACCINE

Hate is a pandemic that has a cure
Simple in words, complex in action
We need healing love now more than ever.
Inoculate Love, Eradicate Hate.

HUNGRY WOLVES

Friend me the dreamers,
The risk takers,
The ones with that idea in their head bursting to take flight,
The ones that have battled, been bruised,
and maybe still clawing and crawling
Yet still manage to decorate their beautiful faces with a smile
or at least hold onto their light.
The light, life has been asking them to put out.
Because they know the human condition
is less about what's on the outside,
And a little more about the hungry wolves on the inside,
waiting to be fed by the meals of their desires.

INTERNET TALES

We have a lot to learn from the trees and the skies

Not just the screens attached to our eyes

How did we get so far from our roots?

How do we move forward in our truths?

We must push past the pain so that we can grow

I wish more for the current world we know.

THE PRIVILEGE OF A HOSPICE VOLUNTEER

She told me I looked like sunshine
coming through the window

She smiled and took her last breath while I held her hand
Who was I to have
the privilege of helping walk her home

You don't know lonely
unless you're faced with the opportunity
Of learning what it means to die alone

NEW MOON
dark days

REARRANGED FURNITURE

My head understands you are gone
but my heart will never let you go.
There's a home for you in my heart.
The memories are like furniture
I rearrange from time to time,
until I find a comfortable seat.

A NIGHT WISH

My favorite part of going to sleep is the hope
I just might get to see you in my dreams.

A MOMENT'S DEFINITION

The day your cape was traded in for wings,
changed my life forever.
From that day on, life could only be defined by
life with you and life after you.

SETTLING INTO PAIN

Even the sun couldn't burn off this kind of pain.
It could only be settled with the moon and the stars.
There is something about the quiet of the night sky
that lets you know it's listening.

FAVORITE STAR

How many nights I shouted at the sky,
envying the stars that hold your light.
In the same breath,
I thank my lucky star knowing it's you.

CAR TALKS

In the car, in my head, in the quiet of the morning
and the late-night walks with the moon.
All the places I go to try and connect with you.
What I wouldn't give to be able to have just one
hour to sit with you.
To ask how you are and see what you have been up to.
To tell you how much I love you and miss you,
how grateful I am to have had you in my life.
No amount of time would be enough and I'm not certain
I would be selfless enough to return you to the stars.
My only solace is in the knowing you hear me,
never missing a beat and giving signs on the days
I need your strength the most.
Your gentle reminders, our loved ones never stop protecting us,
even from the other side.

TIME IS RELATIVE

There is no limit on time as you heal through grief.

And I don't know if I'll ever accept,

the term heal as it relates to grief.

You heal from a broken arm.

You heal from a wound or a cut.

I don't think you can heal from the loss

of someone you love.

The unavoidable pain stays with you on your journey

With the understanding

You learn to carry it, in a smaller bag.

ACHING WARMTH

You are not forgotten, and you never will be,

but sometimes I kid myself

that I'm doing okay without you.

And like the winter cold on bare skin, it hits,

suffocating.

That pain comes fast and swift and there's nowhere to go.

So, I sit in the cold and ache

until the light of your memories brings me warmth again.

HOLLOWS OF GRIEF

I hit play on your only saved message today.
Admittedly, searching for some kind of clue,
Some type of message from the other side.
I come up with nothing.
If I just close my eyes to listen, secretly hoping the
Strength of my memories would have the ability to bring you
back to life.
These are just dreams that rise
As my realities descend to the hollows of grief.

THE CHAIR

When a loved one passes
Deciding what items to keep and what to let go is
an ongoing battle
You know holding onto the items won't bring them back
But there are memories and moments tied to
these everyday items.
One thing is certain,
I will never let go of "the Chair."
Of all the places I've lived, that was your seat,
where you read the paper
And where we shared our chats and thoughts on life
The chair taking notes on your non-judgmental ear,
and your sagely advice
No, I will not part with the chair.
Wherever I may go it comes with me
Wherever I go
You will always have a seat in my home.

NO DRY EYE

Grief is unforgiving
Just when you think there's not a tear left to cry
And your soul has run dry
A song, a picture in your phone or an unassuming
moment will cause of a tidal wave of grief to grab
ahold of your throat and steal your breath
And just when you find your lungs starting to work again
You are pouring lost moments, memories and pain
from each corner of your eye
until you are dehydrated from a lost love
And the cycle repeats again.

THE JOKER

The trouble with grief is it rejects shelter.

There's no place to put it and there is no place to hide.

You play every card in your deck to avoid it.

Yet the Joker returns and no one is laughing.

HONOR WALK

You won't be with me on the day I wear white,
but I will walk with honor wearing your light.

FATHER

The things I hate the most are when "the forgets" start

Forgetting the sound of your voice

Or the way your million-dollar smile

used to light up a room

Forgetting your brevity in a text response

Forgetting how it felt to sit at the dining room table

and read the paper with you

Our unspoken routine

You, reading the sports page and passing me the fashion section

with that signature side smile grin.

I never thanked you for making the coffee,

Something you only did when your kids would visit

just so we could have something that belonged to only us

Coffee no longer tastes the same

and I would give anything to have just one more cup with you

I grab a paper wherever I can and read it,

because you can't

There are people I haven't met yet who will lose out

by not knowing you

And it hurts like hell to know sometimes God calls

his angels home early

Before we're ready to hang up the call

I want to be angry

but the only saving grace is knowing

I was lucky to have you at all

LOVE FROM AFAR

Where do you fly?

What do you see?

Do you still think of me?

Do my tears make you sad?

Remembering all that we had

An angel on earth

Gone too soon

I swear some nights I see your face in the moon

So, I stay up all night

Hoping to connect with your light

You are all around

When your song plays on the radio

Or the chirping cardinal that visits my backyard post

The unexplainable energy that my animals seem to see

I know it's you and I thank you for visiting me

I hope you are happy and now pain free

Your visitation dreams assure me that's your reality

I thank the heavens for all that you are

I will always love you, though now it's love from afar

EMPTY SEAT

There's an empty seat at the holidays
A space missing from an energy large enough
to fill an entire room
It would only stand to reason the emptiness is now
enough to quiet a whole house
Over time we learned to laugh again and continue
to love, some days even dance
Not in exchange for forgetting you but in effort to
maintain your essence

BANDAGE

And tonight, I'll place these hands over your heart.
I can't promise it will help the pain, but I hope it will
stop the bleeding.

MIND WAR

This smile rages war with my head.
Silent battles you will never see.

SMILING IS MY SUPERPOWER

Smiling is my superpower.
It has the ability to brighten your bad day
while simultaneously masking my own.

BLURRY FEELINGS

It is both a blessing and a curse to feel so deeply.
The line between your feelings and my own is blurred.
Some days I don't know who these tears belong to.

EMPTY TANK

I'm exhausted

From trying to run from you

I'm exhausted

From trying to run from me

I'm exhausted

My foot on the gas but the speedometer doesn't move

I'm exhausted

With nothing left to lose

I'm exhausted

From this constant, looming black cloud

I'm exhausted

By what this mirror keeps telling me

I'm exhausted

And dying to be set free

I'm exhausted

From this brain always swimming so deep

I'm exhausted

So, for now I will just sleep

MAYBE NEXT TIME

I know the words to this song by heart

The melancholic tune on repeat

Immobile without energy except enough to make

this pillow flip

Can't get to the cool side fast enough

Because, at least for now, warmth is not welcome.

Not while this song is playing.

Not in this head and not at this moment.

Maybe tomorrow I'll try again.

Maybe tomorrow, I'll get out of bed.

Maybe tomorrow, I'll get out of my head.

STELLAR MOOD

She is as sharp and complex as a diamond's edge

There is not a box in this world big enough for her spirit

To know her was to wonder,

which version you would meet

You could try asking the moon,

but it would only smile at such an inquiry

For she was a constellation of emotions and called

on the appropriate star as her mood dictated.

A HAUNTING

It wasn't the darkness or the spirits
Or the whispering winds that haunted her
Not the late-night howls
Nor the monster under her bed.
Most nights the monsters left her alone.
Torment on hold while her unsettled brain worked
to detangle her spider-web thoughts
So, they crept back under the floorboard
admittedly a little in fear of the monster on the bed
Why carry out a haunting when it already
manifested inside her head?

FOREIGN LANGUAGE

I had been in fight-or-flight mode for so long,
settling into peace has felt like learning a foreign language.

THIS SKIN IS NOT MINE

I'm tired of telling everyone I'm fine
But the truth is I'm not sure this skin is mine

I want to scratch it off, I'm uncomfortable in this space
My mind movies play in the same damn place

In the corner of my brain that won't let me be
Some days I want out of this misery

I look for ways to shut out the noise
Wine, sex, and whiskey but they're only a ploy

But you can't outsmart depression
Or outrun its growing repression

The black cloud lingers
And its deafening voice

I will keep fighting until this skin feels like home
First these invading thoughts need to leave me alone.

FERRIS WHEEL

I don't fear death

It is one of the few things in life that's guaranteed

And for an anxious mind, certainties are appreciated

What I do fear are the breaths from wasted lungs

The ones that do their job but the body that encases them

Never fully learns what it means to be alive

One last ride has a different meaning,

when you are on a Ferris wheel.

START LINE

The in-between space of where you are and where
you want to be can be daunting
I sprinted to get over my hurdles,
tripping over them constantly
It got to the point I had to begin again so many times,
I'm not sure I ever really started.

EASY SMILE

People often told her that she made life look easy.
It was in those moments she learned maybe it was best,
to not always trust a smiling face.

DREAMING AWAKE

And somedays it feels like she's fighting for her life.

Not the one she's living.

But the one she carries out in her dreams.

NOT QUITE WHOLE

I'm somewhere between not quite broken and not quite whole.

GRAY ZONE

I'm aware life is not black or white, yet it is taking time to learn to sit comfortably with the gray.

THE WARDEN

There is no prison more dangerous,
than the one inside your mind.
To be locked away while staring at the key
is pure madness.
So, I write, and I write until my pen runs dry
Trading my pen for the key.

CHAOS

She used to thrive in chaos

Her brain told her there was no other way

But her heart searched a different narrative to convey

THE PROBLEM

The thing about trying to evade pain is how it will eventually

show up in all the ways you try to hide it.

And before you know it,

your pain has become a problem.

CRASHED HOPE

I had strived to be like water for so long,

To ebb and flow like the tide,

To gracefully dance over the rocks until

They smoothed over by the coming and going

of my waves.

But I am merely the boat in the eye of the storm

Crashing into the rocks,

much like crashing into my own hope.

LONELY

I don't mind the solace of my own company.

But the heart is so much lighter,

when someone else is helping to hold it up.

WEARY TRAVELER

These late nights hold me still

As I continue to wonder

How long must this soul travel?

How many more holes in these shoes until

My arms are wrapped around you.

WILL YOU WAIT?

Some days I feel as if you are off in some corner

Silently cheering me on

With a sign, I can't yet see

But it has my name on it and reads "keep going."

And your shadow fills in when I hold onto hope

And then your shadow gets darker when I drop the rope

Of this invisible thread from you to me.

Waiting on divine intervention and waiting on me

Because you let go of your past and the pain

And I'm still drowning in my own rain

Clawing and digging out of this hole

With your umbrella nearby for my shattered soul.

And like Mary Poppins I want to fly to you

Because I believe in true love

and my dreams will come through.

I will keep praying for your sign I cannot yet see

But for now, I hope you can read mine.

It says, "will you wait for me?"

ALIEN

She was not from this planet
Of that she was certain
But she holds on.
Waiting for the day he finds her heart,
and finally takes her home.

DREAM

As the stars align with heaven above,

praying to God to give me a reason to understand true love.

WAXING CRESCENT
gaining light

FIGHTER

She had a little bit of fight left and that's all she needed to get back in the ring.

BLOOD THIRST

When toxic people can no longer access you,

they'll get desperate for just one more drink of your supply.

Cut them off and let them thirst.

They cannot open locked doors to which they have no keys.

OPENED EYES

It feels as though some days,

this heavy heart is too big for this body.

However, I take comfort in the knowing that

when my time is up

it can be said with the sincerest honesty,

it will be the first time these eyes fully close.

SHATTERED MOLD

The thing is darling, this mold you created
was only ever made for me to break.

RESTED

Then one morning I woke rested.
The first time I recognized,
I slept better without than with you.
And in that moment
I knew there is peace in making the right choice,
even if it hurts

HEALING WOUNDS

You didn't choose these wounds, but you get to
decide you're healing.

OVERSIZED SWEATSHIRT

It's not that pain escapes me.

It's just instead of wearing pain

like my favorite oversized sweatshirt,

It is now draped over the chair next to me.

I see it and appreciate it.

But I recognize its time to do some laundry.

This isn't the only piece of clothing I own and

It might be possible to find peace in other feelings now,

Even if the tags are still on.

MAP TO NOWHERE

You will soon unfold

the version of me that is no longer home.

Search all you want,

but you will only encounter

empty roads and vacant homes.

MIND CHATTER

There is inspiration in the noise.
Chaos is not found in the source,
but in deciding what noise to turn down
and which ones to turn all the way up.

LOVE STORY

I was in love with a lie.

And the lie was me.

Falling in love with a new soul.

Her name is Truth.

BROKEN REARVIEW

Even if your feet can't move right now,
make sure your eyes are looking forward.

MELANCHOLY SMILE

She had a sunshine smile

with bouts of melancholy

and to acknowledge one side would be futile.

As one side made art,

and the other learned to appreciate it.

Mother Nature taught her this.

If you need proof,

remember what the sun can do at the end of a storm.

DON'T BREAK

Let the tears fall
Let them cleanse you
And as needed let them change you
But, darling, no matter what
Don't let them break you.

IRONIC LOVE

The cruel irony of letting go of something
you loved so much,
Is that you eventually learn to combat that pain with love.
To love yourself in a way
you may have otherwise not understood.

LOVE SYRUP

If love is a drug, maybe I've spent too much time dispensing it
to the wrong people.
Perhaps it's time to take a taste of my own medicine.

FALLING HIGHER

The problem with the perfectionist's path to

healing is an all or nothing approach is destined for failure

Realign with the notion it may take you more than

one try, one month, one year, one decade

To get out of wherever you're feeling stuck.

Start digging, you will fall, you will stumble

But each time you will learn a little bit more about

your bruises and scars along the way.

They have a story to tell you if choose to listen,

Each a roadmap to where you're destined next

Do not equate roadblocks,

self-induced or external with being stuck

or that you'll never get the lead out of your legs

Every time you fall, rise higher.

Eventually, my love, the rise will feel better than the fall.

NEW BLOOD

The erroneous idea that is has closed too soon
Is the problem with healing an open wound
Injury implemented years before
And your pouring of salt
Won't settle the score
Take all the time if that's what you need
But rip the Band-Aid so you can bleed
Bleed out the poison and leave it ajar
One day, you'll showcase your beautiful scar

THE FLIGHT

These thoughts
The ones that keep knocking on my door
They can show up all they want
But they can't ground me anymore
I've found my wings and it's time to fly
I'll wave to these weighted thoughts
from my freedom in the sky

CONTRADICTION

I'm a walking contradiction
I drink cold pressed juice followed by a shot of tequila

I'll never apologize for being myself
But apologies if I've ever made you feel less than yourself

I cry between my smiles
I love with all my heart

Try to send it back to me and I'll question your motive
But I'm learning to accept love the way it should
arrive, warm, unattached, and without limitations

I love animals more than most people
With the exception of my family and friends
and strangers that bare a bit of their soul in
unexpected exchanges

I hate being cold
But love the way my hiking boots sound as they
crunch through winter snow on a moonlit hike

The thought of being tired exhausts me
But I'll pull an all-nighter to watch the sunset and
sunrise in the same breath

I despise the sticky feeling of bug spray on my skin
However, I challenge that a cold beer on a starry,
summer night will never taste as good as in that moment

I'm not a fan of confrontation but call me to the fire
And I promise, you will never win a verbal argument with me

I'm an Aries to my core
But I don't subscribe to the zodiac,

I see myself in all the signs
As well as myself in a little bit of everyone I meet

When someone asks me if I am a morning or evening person
I say, "it depends on the day."

I prefer late night hugs from the moon
But some days, there is nothing like being kissed by the sun.

And that is why I'll forever be a walking contradiction,
Dancing to the beat of my own drum.

ORDINARY PEOPLE

We are but ordinary people playing out characters in
Extraordinary scenes,
Wondering why we can't cope.
Maybe it was to teach us how to hold onto hope
These frayed ribbons from our hearts to the soul
Indelible life moments reminding us
To keep holding on and never let go.

UNBOTHERED

I'm beginning to question if snakes really have spines.

All the ones I know don't.

Excuse me, your rattle is showing and I'm unbothered.

Tell the Devil it was a wasted trip.

My faith flies louder than your rattle's shake.

RED HEAD

I've been different
Always "that girl with the red hair"
I've been called every redhead name in the book
From fire crotch to carrot top,
mind you, from complete strangers.
In my younger years, I was often told
I was pretty, "for a redhead."

I remember as a child despising summer and the
shedding of clothes
Cringing making my entrance from the pool house
out to the pool
A little too conscious
of my glowing pale skin and freckles
I knew everyone would be staring,
as I did my white skin walk of shame.
Expectantly waiting for more comments from
complete strangers reminding me of the mutant that I was.

Back then, I would use smelly sunless tanners
in pursuit of blending in,
but something about the combination of sun, pale
skin and freckles somehow makes you whiter.
In college, while sporting a tank top, a man once
came up to me at a bar and told me that I looked
like someone put a porch screen in front of me and
threw dirt on me, referencing my arm freckles.

I heard comments like this my whole life.
Most innocent teases, some more intentional.
I apologized to myself more times than I can count,
just for being different.
After a while I began to believe
my difference was my weakness.

But then one day that changed.

I can't remember when or how,
But I came to the understanding that being a part of only

two percent of the world's population
doesn't make me wrong, it makes me rare.
And in a copycat world I've learned to embrace my
scattered specs and vibrant hue as they are a part
of my story and they were created from love.

My hair color may be a part of who I am,
but I am so much more
Behind my hair and skin lies the DNA of Mexican,
French, German and Welsh heritage
Let my looks and last name be a walking a
reminder to never judge a book by its cover
Which is why I vow to never judge the looks of another

I don't apologize for me and I won't deny myself or my genes
ever again
Like the red hair queen I am
I shine proudly with this crown of Pheomelanin.

*Pheomelanin (type of pigment that causes red hair)

DANDELION IN BLOOM

A weed teaches us you can grow up
where you don't belong,
and still blossom into a beautiful flower.

ELOQUENT MOTHER

Some days Mother Nature holds my pen.

Her beauty is far more eloquent,

than any words I could ever write.

WELCOME HOME

Mother Nature knows all my secrets,
yet she welcomes me home anyway.

YOUR TIME IS COMING

Do not judge yourself for what you feel.
Acknowledge your thoughts so you can heal.
Just like flowers die and bloom again,
someday you will too, my beautiful friend.

LOVE PALETTE

I'm a little in love with the way Mother Nature paints.
Her ability to transform an entire scene
into an absolute relic,
without using any words at all.

MOON WHISPERS

Perhaps it was these wine-soaked lips

Or the seductive dance of the orange and yellow flames from

the open pit fire

But I'm not discounting a little magic happened that night

A quiet moment between the moon and I

Shining bright in the late summer sky

Maple and Oak offering a peak under their leaves

The nights cool air calling for sleeves

And as that roaring fire continued to burn

The moon whispered that soon, I'll understand

Why I've been waiting my turn.

QUEEN BEE

Oh, Little Queen Bee
Flying in your honey dripped colony.
Your soldiers dance around you, dear,
Unaware you are the one they should fear
One sting from the queen bee
Don't misstep, she doesn't love easily
Treat her kind because she'll make your kingdom grow
With the understanding,
There's only one queen bee you'll ever know.

ROOTED

I've always admired the way trees dance,
gracefully in the wind,
Standing ancestrally proud and rooted in the earth
as their branches sway back and forth
while mother nature plays her melodic wind whispers.

It is like she's sending a secret song,
that speaks to every branch and leaf of the tree.
And there's no noise loud enough to replace her tune

What it must be like to be so grounded by your roots,
that you can move freely, at your own pace
without having to ask permission from anyone or anything.

DICHOTOMY

Such a dichotomy—logic and creativity.
Logic never stays up late talking to the moon,
and creativity isn't inspired by coloring in the lines.

LESSONS FROM MY NEPHEW

You are allowed to accept your broken pieces
To fashion them together in whatever design fits you
How unimaginative would Legos be,
If they arrived already put together?

TRUTH TALKS

You are beautiful, you have purpose, and you are loved
And I mean this from every corner of my heart
But, they are just words until you believe it yourself.
Start by agreeing to agree there might be some
Truth to these words and grow from there.

WRITTEN IN THE STARS

My love, is it possible?
You've been walking alone for so long,
So that your eyes can remain open to see
What's written in the stars for you?

BONE STORIES

Etched in my bones are stories of sin
Writing them one by one to let the healing begin
I've seen love and I've come to know loss
In my efforts to avoid loneliness at all costs
Sometimes the things we fight the most
End up being the most noticeable ghosts
Forced to face these as I became undone
Lovingly stitching myself back together
The best is yet to come

LEMONADE

There may come a time when life hands you so
many lemons you become allergic to lemonade.
You just want to fold, let go, give up.
You're losing your grip and your hands are tired.
Your soul is heavy, and your heart is weary.
You just want someone to save you
or pass by unnoticed at all.
This, this spot right here
is where I'm going to need you to do something.
I'm going to need you to not let go.
If that's all you can do.
Set your feet down on something firm and look up.
Find the closest mirror you have and look at yourself in the eye
and tell yourself these 5 things:

1) I am a warrior
2) I give myself grace and the understanding of doing the
    best I could with the tools and resources I had at the time
3) I acknowledge and understand that being a good

person does not exempt me from the pain and perils from life

4) I promise to protect my heart and spirit first from this day forward

5) I deserve happiness

Envision the youngest version of yourself that you can remember and tell that sweet baby that they are safe, they are loved, and you will protect them from this day forward. Repeat this once a day, every day, for as long as you need, until you can stomach the taste of lemonade again.

I don't write these words to tell you what to do
I write these words to let you know, I've battled too.

FULL MOON
shining bright

UNFINISHED PAGES

You don't have a title for it yet,
because your story isn't finished.

SHADOWS OF THE PAST

How can you let the sun in when you are hanging
onto the shadows of your past?

COLOR-BLIND

I hope when the dust settles, you are surrounded
by people who help you see life in color.

FAIRYTALES

No matter how much life has hardened you,
honor the parts that still believe in fairytales.

THE SURRENDER

There will come a time in your life where surrendering to the pause will be more meaningful then pressing play.

DAY DREAMER

It's okay to call me the girl with her head in the clouds.

Day dreaming is where I go to meet the people and places

I've yet to experience.

Inspiration for where my feet should go next.

WINDY ROADS

Of all the roads she has traveled, the one back to herself has been the longest.

LAUNCH PAD

How remarkable is the evolution of the things that were *meant to fly*.

ALBUM RELEASE

Maybe heartache was the song I needed to hear in order to write my own album.

HEART BEAT

And so, the road proved
to be a bit bumpier than anticipated.

But that was okay because she was okay.

This time she believed it,
because this time she was living it.

The road wasn't any smoother,
but her ability to adapt was found in letting go

And letting the beating object, feel something for once.

THE WALK

The bridge between what is no longer a home
and where you want to be can be a cold, solitary walk.
Hope and faith are the light of the path and I can't
wait to get to the other side with those two by my side.

WHITE-KNUCKLE RIDE

The ups and downs of life are a guarantee.

How we handle them are not

I am so sick and tired of that white-knuckling life.

Roller coasters are more fun with your hands up anyway.

WILD VEINS

With wildflowers in her veins,
she learned to dance in the rain.
For she is as spontaneous as she is free.

LATE BLOOMER

My life, it may not look like yours
And for the longest,
I played the dangerous comparison game
My neck turned so far from myself
Watering someone else's life with my own tears
But just because my garden was only seeds at the time,
it didn't make me any less of one
It's then that I realized something about late bloomers.
Because they may take a little more time to grow,
sometimes their roots run a little deeper.

LETTERS TO MY YOUNGER SELF

You had dreams in your heart once
One's seen through the eyes
of naive promise and excitement
When did you stray so far from that little girl?
It's time to go back and do what's best for you
Promise me, baby girl, you'll see
her childhood dreams through.

FOUR-WALLED CHAMBERS

Our hearts communicate the loudest.

Inside those four-walled chambers holds the truth.

Let it speak its truth and as it beats, let it be from love.

SHAPESHIFTER

She's always resonated with the clouds,
shape shifting into whatever the world needed of her.
How powerful to uncover,
her rain of tears could block the sun for a while
and still have the ability to make things grow.
Validating, rain can be a persuasive catalyst,
for things that look to the sun.

THE MANTRA

Focus on what you are chasing

and never forget your why

Commit to your future,

but be patient with your when

Dedicate your life to *grow, grow, grow*

Desire to make it happen so you can *glow, glow, glow*

KRYPTONITE

Do not try to read me,

or put me in a box.

I'm not afraid to be opened.

It's just you'll learn that I can't be contained.

Fire needs to breathe,

and glass ceilings are my kryptonite.

NINE LIVES

Sometimes you have to die to learn what it means to live.

I'm fairly certain, I am in fact, part cat.

ADVENTUROUS TONGUE

Dehydrated with a thirst for adventure,
A trip to the moon offered her a sip of its light for
her parched tongue.
Showered in echoes of moonbeams and shooting
stars they promised she'd never go thirsty again
And she vowed to never return the same.

LIMITS

I don't have limits except for the ones that belong to boundaries.

UNHINGED

Let it come unhinged

Let it come unglued

Splatter

Shatter

Then find something that matters

And never let it go

The person, the thought,

The movement.

Whatever it is that sparks your soul

You didn't happen by accident

And neither did your purpose

If your world is falling apart right now,

Take a seat, hold on tight and get ready to rise

The sun is calling you home.

You can step into your light now.

It has been waiting for you.

VOLITION

She was occupied with a little more volition

and a little less superstition

It didn't mean she no longer believed in magic

It just meant she now knew,

which direction to point her wand.

THE WAIT

She craved a love that was free, full of life, and laughter
A love that carried her through dark days
And celebrated her light days
A love where the fire of two old souls
Kept warmth for the hands of the other
A love that was etched in the moon,
when they were merely stars
Traced by the promises of its shine
And when their eyes met,
time had a way of slowing down
Gratitude embedded in the deepest parts of their hearts
With the unspoken knowing that it was all worth the wait

THE COMPASS

Tucked away or shining bright
Is an internal compass stored in your light
The thoughts and ideas that brighten its bulb
Those are the ideas rooted in love
Dig your heels and follow that light
And no matter what happens,
you'll never lose your sight

BAREFOOT MOON WALKS

Barefoot and enraptured, she walked amongst the stars.
The curious moon whispered to the stars,
"Why does she walk on her tip toes?"
To which they replied, "To avoid waking the sun."

OVERDUE

She was due for a happy chapter.

PUT YOUR OXYGEN MASK ON FIRST

Of all the people you choose to beg to stay in your life,

make sure it's the best version of yourself,

who's pants you tug on first.

DNA TOOLBOX

You were placed here,

plucked from God's green garden.

Perfect in your imperfections.

No one promised life would be easy

These scuffs, these bruises are a part of your plan.

You are not being punished,

only learning how to take a stand

The more you stand in your truths,

the more you awaken your gifts.

Not the ones you admire about your neighbor,

but the ones instilled in your DNA.

As unique to you as you are to this world.

Open your gifts and share your light.

There's a star in the night sky with your name on it

And it's begging you to mirror its shine.

HOPE IN A HAND

Sometimes we sit uncomfortably in the dark with
no access to light except for the one called hope.
It is the flashlight of life that will always guide our way.
The trick is to not let go.

DEAR GOD

I hope with all my heart,

that the person reading these words see their value.

No matter how small they feel or what they have been through,

Please open their timid hearts to let them know

beautiful moments are in store for them too.

ENOUGH

And maybe today, I'll just rest in this moment.

With no expectation of self, of life.

Just knowing that I am enough,

and *this too shall pass.*

TWILIGHT MAGIC

There's magic in the twilight.

The thin veil between the past and the present

The opposition of both light and the dark

The space where a tired soul and a renewed spirit meet and

exchange stories

Where the handoff between one another holds both an

understanding and a promise of what

We can and cannot control.

And I'm certain, the silent surrender at this crossroad is what it

means to understand life.

THE SOURCE

Even in the darkest of days,

there is a pilot light that lives inside us.

That, my friend, is called the source.

No matter how dark it gets, do not, under any circumstances,

put that light out.

You may not feel it now, but someday

There will be someone, something or some idea that will

cause a spark to ignite and relight your fire.

Hold on, it's coming.

"To see life in its sincerest form of beauty, one must observe it through the written words from the souls of poets." -E.W.

In my heart, I believe we all have a little bit of poet in us. I left these next few pages blank and available for you, to write your story, as you see fit.

A few questions to prompt your story should you need some light:

- What do you need right now?
- What are you most proud of?
- What do you love most about yourself?
- What areas in your life have you feeling stuck?
- What does life look like if you continue on your current path?
- What are you struggling to let go of?
- What do you wish to tell your younger self?
- What do you wish to tell your future self?
- What do you want to be your story?

AUTHOR BIO

E.W. Rightings is the soul spirit and nom de plume of author Carrie Gonzales. Carrie a native from Detroit, MI with stopping points in NYC. She currently resides in Cleveland, OH with her dog, Daisy, and cat, Gatsby. Carrie is a Registered Dietitian and an Integrative Nutrition Health Coach. She enjoys helping others live their best life through nutrition and beyond. In her spare time, Carrie enjoys photography, the great outdoors, cooking, and spending time with loved ones.

If you would like to learn further, follow and connect with her on Instagram: @ew_rightings or cegwellness@gmail.com.

Made in the USA
Monee, IL
28 December 2020

55699627R00111